Voice of Babasaheb Ambedkar

"Most people in India do not make constructive suggestions. The reason is not that there are not people capable of constructive thought. The reason why all constructive thought remain bottled up is because a long and continuous propaganda has inculcated upon the minds of the generality of the people that nothing should be respected and nothing should be accepted unless it emanates from a [particular] group of people."

-Bhimrao Ambedkar

VOICE OF BABASAHEB AMBEDKAR

Dr. Ravindra Kumar
Mrs. Kamlesh Kumar

Translated By
Megha and Sachin Arora

GYAN PUBLISHING HOUSE
NEW DELHI-110002

Voice of Babasaheb Ambedkar

ISBN : 81-212-0934-X

Rs. 360

Published in 2007 in India by

Gyan Publishing House

5, Ansari Road, Darya Ganj, New Delhi-110002

Phones: 23261060, 23282060, Fax: ++91-11-23282060

E-mail: books@gyanbooks.com

Laser Typesetting at: **Naresh Computers**

Printed at: **Salasar Imaging System, New Delhi**

CONTENTS

****

FOREWORD

Babasaheb Dr. Bhimrao Ambedkar had a dynamic personality. He not only raised voice and worked for the upliftment of the downtrodden and the oppressed but also made a memorable contribution as a leader of revolution in society.

Babasaheb Ambedkar was a progressive thinker. Equality and justice had always been nucleus in his thoughts and all through his life he fought for them unconditionally. A person like Babasaheb does not get birth commonly.

Babasaheb was a great Indian; he was a true patriot and was in favour of assuring the contribution of all in the progress of the country. He had clear thoughts about economy and politics; he was strongly in favour of honest, clean and value-based public life.

Babasaheb not only gave his priceless and unforgettable contribution to the making of the Constitution of Indian Republic but also served the nation by becoming a member of the first cabinet of independent India.

Babasaheb Ambedkar wished to see India strong and safe on all sides. Therefore, he stressed on clear policies, internal and external, and notified the policy makers from time to time in this regard.

It is a matter of great pleasure that Dr. Ravindra Kumar and Mrs. Kamlesh Kumar have prepared this manuscript from social, cultural, political and economic views of Babasaheb Dr. Bhimrao Ambedkar. No doubt, after publication, this work will introduce general readers with the priceless and worth adopting thoughts of Babasaheb. They will learn a lot from them and would know their duties towards society and nation; and would come ahead to fulfil the mission of establishing of equality and justice as per the hope of Babasaheb.

I congratulate Dr. Ravindra Kumar and Mrs. Kamlesh Kumar for their efforts and wish for the success of this publication.

—K. R. Narayanan

SELF-UTTERANCE

For years, it had been my desire to prepare books on great nation-builders. In this chain, except some biographies, I worked on some front-ranking leaders of the Subcontinent on the basis of historical truths. Side-by-side, I also prepared manuscripts for general readers on Sardar Vallabhbhai Patel, Netaji Subhas Chandra Bose, Swami Vivekananda and Lokamanya Bal Gangadhar Tilak. It had been my effort to especially make general readers acquainted of the exemplary and worthy views expressed time-to-time by these leaders on the various issues related to culture, society, education, politics, religion and economy. In this very series some time ago my brother Mr. Lakhmendra Khurana requested me to bring out a work on Dr. Bhimrao Ambedkar also. Consequently, the next manuscript, in this series is ready on Babasaheb. Like other manuscripts, this has also been finalized with the help of Kamlesh by extracting from the speeches, essays, statements and letters of Dr. Ambedkar.

The intelligence, deep analyzing method and positive attitude of Dr. Ambedkar should be considered unique. He was a scholar and was not less than any other cotemporary scholar.

It is true that Ambedkar did not altogether write on those burning issues that were important in social, political and economic fields in his time and were eligible for analysis and solution, but it is quite important that the topics he chose from them were directly related to the people who had been poor and oppressed for thousands of years. The future of millions of downtrodden was related to them. In Ambedkar's views those subjects were not less important than political independence of India. Definitely in this regard he was right to a great extent.

The articles he presented, after a deep analysis and intensive research, on Untouchability, Caste-System and the origin of Shudras, are the proof of his unique intelligence. Not only this, his writings on economic and political subjects, his views pertaining to legislation and comments he made from time to time in this regard were unique in themselves. Even today, his articles, views and comments are equally relevant.

Babasaheb Ambedkar openly wrote on land and land-reform, size of holdings and related-problems, non-profitable labour and labourer and industrial disputes, trade unions and related issues. He brought to light the problems related to these subjects and presented ideas of solving them. He favoured for constitutional reforms, educational reforms and general law to be made meaningful for all, which was important and still is.

II

Dr. Ambedkar did not take part in the national liberation movement for India. Why? He himself had disclosed the reasons in many of his articles, speeches and statements. This is up to the readers to analyze his arguments honestly. But I have no hesitation in saying that Babasaheb Ambedkar was a great patriot. He needs no certificate to prove his love for India. This point is cleared by the several quotes from his thoughts, articles, speeches and statements, included in this book; still, I would like to quote some of his sayings here.

Like a great and true national leader, Ambedkar said in February 1942, ***"I have dispute with the communal Hindus over some points, but I swear before you that I will submit my life for the safety of my nation."*** No doubt, this is clear from his statement that Babasaheb was not only the leader of ***Dalits***, but also of the whole nation. I will again say that he was a great patriot. Like a great nationalist and front-ranking leader, he asked for self-rule based on equality, not only for ***Dalits*** but also for each and every Indian. This was fully justified, essential and along with being the need of time, it was also very important for the unity, stability and integrity of the nation.

Ambedkar should be considered a revolutionist in the social field. Such a revolutionary never compromised with issues of national interests. When a critical situation arose with regards of the merger of the Hyderabad State into the Union of India, and when Nizam was dreaming of freeing the State by getting involved in anti-Indian activities, at that time, the message Ambedkar conveyed to the ***Dalits*** of Hyderabad can enlighten many. Babasaheb said to the ***Dalits*** of Hyderabad that they should never think of supporting such a ruler [Nizam], who is anti-Indian, no matter if they might have many complaints with Casteist Hindus.

The Caste-System has divided the nation. Caste-System has been the cause of social disintegration. That is why I myself agree with Babasaheb's thoughts in regard of Caste-System. Although I do not fully agree with his analysis about the origin of the ***Shudras***, still I am much impressed by his interpretation of the issue The main thing in this regard is that in his full interpretation, Ambedkar considers ***Aryans*** to be Indian and not the foreigners.

Much has been said about differences between Mahatma Gandhi and Babasaheb Ambedkar. Much is said in regards of the way of actions of both. Both had difference of opinion and their ways of working were also different. This is true. Therefore, I do not wish to discuss it here, each and everyone can do so according to his own viewpoint. However, I will say that Dr. Ambedkar respected Mahatma Gandhi. Babasaheb never denied the works and efforts done by Mahatma Gandhi for the ***Dalits*** and ***Untouchables***. A great personality like Ambedkar could never do that. Yes, the truth is that Babasaheb Ambedkar considered the work or efforts of Mahatma Gandhi for the ***Dalits*** and ***Untouchables*** as insufficient. Therefore, there were differences of opinion between them, which were natural. This was also because that the basis of the viewpoints of Babasaheb had been intensive research and analysis and along with that he had some bitter experiences of his life in his own country. These experiences could be gained only by those who have been into them.

Today, it is the need of hour that each Indian should follow the views and works of Babasaheb Ambedkar. He is worthy of the respect and honour of all Indians and not of only one community. Any Indian, speaking unnecessarily against him, virtually challenges his own patriotism and love for the nation. It should be remembered that Babasaheb Ambedkar was the Voice of India; he was a true representative of national approach. He was the forbearer of social reform.

In translating this manuscript from Hindi into English, Megha and Sachin Arora have assisted me greatly. Along with this, Mr. Sachin Bathla, Dr. Bani Benarjee, Dr. S. Vincent De Paul, Mr.

Mrinal Khurana and Dr. Rana Purushottam Kumar Singh have extended their help especially making the manuscript error free by proof reading. I convey my hearty thanks to all of them.

–Ravindra Kumar

23-B, Lane: 2, Mansarovar
Civil Lines, Meerut-250001 [India]
Phone: 0091-121-2645551
E-mail: ravindrakumar5@rediffmail.com
ravindrakumar5@hotmail.com
ravindrakumar5@sify.com

TO THE READERS

There can nothing be more tragic if any Indian considers Babasaheb Dr. Bhimrao Ambedkar as the leader of a particular community or tries to minimize his great personality. He talked about ***the Dalits.*** He raised his voice for the ***Untouchables***. He took the side of the poor. All these things are true. But these are the things that are justified too. The person who talks about poor, ***Dalits*** and ***Untouchables***, cannot be a small person. Such a person can only be great. Babasaheb Ambedkar was a great man. His thoughts and works were also great. His name cannot be erased from the history of India. The legacy he left in academic and intellectual field cannot be denied.

Clarity in thoughts, bravery, logic and positive approach were among the main facets of his personality. He was not greedy. He never desired for any important post. But he had never learned to compromise with his ideals. This was not a small thing. This was something to beautify his great and revolutionary life. Along with this, he gave due respect and honour to others. Although Mahatma Jotirao Govindrao Phule was his ideal, still more or less, even after some differences of opinion, his respect was not less for Lokamanya Tilak, Mahatma Gandhi and Sardar Patel too. He also respected Gokhale and Savarkar while Mahadeo Govind Ranade was praised by him.

The life and works of Dr. Ambedkar are the source of inspiration for all of us. Much can be learned from him in respect of unity and consolidation of the nation and society. I believe that the present and the future generations will step forward in this respect. I am proud of helping Dr. Ravindra Kumar in the preparation of this work. In future too I will be supportive to Dr. Kumar in such works.

–Kamlesh Kumar

Meerut, U. P. [India]

"You have found your saviour in Ambedkar. I am confident that he found will break your shackles. Not only that, a time will come when, so whispers my conscience, Ambedkar will shine as a front-rank leader of India fame and appeal."

-Shahuji Maharaj
The Maharaja of Kolhapur
March 21, 1920

BABASAHEB IN VIEW OF CONTEMPORARIES

"No one can hope to make any effective mark upon his time and bring the aid that is worth bringing to great principles and struggling causes if he is not strong in his love and his hatred. I hate injustice; tyranny, pompousness and humbug, and my hatred embrace all those who are guilty of them. I want to tell my critics that I regard my feelings of hatred as a real force."

—Bhimrao Ambedkar

Precious Patriot

"I know that he [Ambedkar] is a precious patriot."

-Mahatma Gandhi

Architect of Constitution

"Ambedkar was the architect of our Constitution, and services rendered by him in various capacities, could not be exaggerated."

-Dr. Rajendra Prasad

Social Reformer

"Ambedkar will be remembered...as the symbol of revolt against all the oppressing features of Hindu Society. His virulent opposition to these oppressive features will keep people's mind awake."

-Pt. Jawaharlal Nehru

Great Scholar

"The troubles Ambedkar faced, perhaps very few amongst us have faced; so learned he is, perhaps very few amongst are..."

-Sardar Vallabhbhai Patel

Honest and Righteous

"Ambedkar was a thoroughly an honest person, a scholar, a righteous man, and his approach was true and with full of consciousness; he was a friend and such a one finds peace after life's fulfils work."

-C. Rajagopalachari

Scholar and a Man of Qualities

"Ambedkar's great intellectual qualities, scholarship and his service to the nation, and his own [*Dalit*] community have put him in the front rank of great man of India."

-B. G. Horniman

A Man of Multi-Dimensional Personality

"Ambedkar's personality, erudition and capacity to lead and organize make him a unique asset of our country."

-Veer Savarkar

A Liberated One

"Ambedkar was a great leader; he served the nation and attained *Nirvana*."

-Bhadanta Ananda Kaushalyana

Illustrious Figure of History

"Ambedkar was one of those illustrious figures who played historical role in the annals of India, especially for the upliftment of the masses."

-U. Nu [Prime Minister of Burma]

A Great Reformer

"Ambedkar struggled for the rights of the depressed classes and suffered. He fought against injustice, oppression and inequality; and he did not revolt against Hinduism, but tried to reform it."

-Acharya P. K. Atre

A Great Missionary

"Ambedkar lived for the achievement of certain values. The aim of his life was quite important and that was directed towards the upliftment of the downtrodden and oppressed people."

-Koyaji

National Leader

"Ambedkar is one of the most learned leaders of the country; he is not only a leader of dalits, but also a leader of India."

-B. G. Kher

Public Servant

"Babasaheb Ambedkar was a great servant [of the people] and [also] a great power; he had the ability to run the Government of India alone."

-S. K. Patil

****

BABASAHEB IN VIEWOF NATIONAL AND INTERNATIONAL PRESS

"As nothing is greater than self-respect and self-pride, the people belong to Scheduled Castes, down-trodden and poor [communities] not withdrawing themselves from these two things and putting their immense labour and through all their capabilities should achieve them. They will get social justice only by doing so, of which they are equally entitled, and through which they will improve their economic conditions."

-Bhimrao Ambedkar

Able Personality

"Ambedkar was an able, gifted and versatile personality, who, in different circumstances, might have rendered even greater services to the nation and society."

-The Times of India

A Man of Letters

"Ambedkar's deep expression in the field of law, and economics, labour, politics and sociology, even in propitious circumstances, made him a towering personality in the world of scholars. His contribution in the world of letters would be memorable for a long."

-The Statesman

A Man of Consciousness

"Ambedkar was such a man of the amazing career, who was bent upon the destruction of the old order which was based on injustice and denial of human rights; he was a worthy son of this continent."

-Amrit Bazar Partika

A Patriot

"He [Ambedkar] is a patriot and desires a complete self-rule [for India]"

-Indian Daily Mail

An Influential Leader

"What will remain in a recollection of his [Ambedkar's] great services to the nation and the impression left on his contemporaries of a vivid and versatile personality."

-The Hindustan Times

An Upright Person

"Ambedkar would be remembered as an upright person; he did revolt against falsehood."

-Free Press Journal

A Revolutionary

"Ambedkar is revolutionary leader of modern India; showing full respect to [***Swamy***] Dayananda, [***Mahatma***] Gandhi and [***Veer***] Savarkar, it can be said that Ambedkar's services to the Untouchables rank higher."

- [Marathi] Prabhat

A Respected Leader

"Ambedkar was known as an honoured leader of Untouchables throughout the world."

-The New York Times

A Great Contributor

"Ambedkar put a profound impression upon India's major legal structure."

-The Times, London

****

"No thinking human being can be tied down to a view once expressed in the name of consistency. More important than consistency is responsibility. A responsible person must learn to unlearn what he has learned. A responsible person must have the courage to rethink and change his thoughts. Of course, there must be good and sufficient reasons for unlearning what he has learned and for recasting his thoughts. There can be no finality in thinking."

-Bhimrao Ambedkar

VOICE OF BABASAHEB

"There is nothing wrong in being grateful to a great man who has rendered life-long service to the country; but there is a limit to gratefulness. As has been well said by the Irish patriot Daniel O'Connell, 'No man can be grateful at the cost of his honour; no woman can be grateful at the cost of her chastity; and no nation can be grateful at the cost of its liberty', this caution is far more necessary in the case of India than in the case of any other country. We have to understand this reality."

-Bhimrao Ambedkar

1
Primitive Society

"No doubt, the primitive society was made of roving and it was not due to the reason that those roving has any hereditary tendency to move about; The society was of roving because in primitive age the animals were the property of men, and because [their property] animals were roving, they too had to become roving."

Social Problems

"Every problem in human society is a social problem; and the use of political power can solve that problem."

Social Status

"The social status of an individual by itself often becomes a source of power."

Social Instinct

"There is nothing to be worried about [social] instincts [***Samskaras***]. Every society grants recognition to them."

Social Distinction

"It should be remembered that the primitive society was made of roving-communities while the modern society consist of [permanently] settled [people's] communities. Along with this, in primitive age tribesmen or the communities of tribesmen were the basis of society while in the modern times society consists of local communities settled in fixed particular regions."

Social Equality

"Hindu Society must be based upon Casteless principle; merely inter-Caste marriages and collective-eating cannot remove Untouchability. Along with this, equality in opportunities in economic and administrative fields is also essential. And practices of political field should be such that one's rights are not violated; equal guarantee is given for the protection of human rights."

Social Change

"It is the change which has brought us from the primitive society to the modern society; this change can be seen from all point of view-economic, political and social."

Social Reform

"The path of social reform, like the path to heaven at any rate in India, is strewn with many difficulties."

Continuity of Change

"Society too is in the scope of change. How is it possible that its hundreds and thousands year's old rules and regulations can be maintained on the basis of this argument that they have been good? If they are to be maintained it is possible only after setting them according to the need of time and circumstances."

Social-Economic Reforms

"Probably, no economic reform is possible unless we bring changes in our social system."

Social Re-Construction

"Before starting work in the direction of social reconstruction we must be well-acquainted of relationship between man and society. It is such a problem which cannot fall into the hands of many social scientists."

Importance of Social Reform

"I regard social reform more fundamental than political reform."

Admiration of Social Reform

"I approve all efforts, small or big, that are made in the direction of social reforms."

Caste and Society

"To bring a revolution in the field of social reform, ultimately, we have to come forward to abolish Caste

[System] though we may not be able to do so at the initial stage."

State and Society

"The words '***State***' and '***Society***' are often presented as though there was a contrast between the two. But there is no distinction of a fundamental character between a State and a Society."

State, Society and Power

"It is true that the plenary powers of the State operate through the sanction of law while society depends upon religious and social sanction for the enforcement of its plenary powers. The fact however remains that both have plenary powers to coerce. As such, there is no contrast between State and Society."

Distinction of State and Society

"The persons composing society are persons who are also members of the State. So, there is no difference between State and Society."

Self-Sufficiency of State

"In my opinion the first condition for a linguistic province to come into being is that it should be self-dependent from economic point of view."

Control on State

"No majority community should misuse the power by wearing the mask of a linguistic province; it is necessary to think of device to inspect and control the province being created in the name of language."

Caste and State

"In reality, the state cannot be made completely free unless the caste system rules upon the society in India."

Significance of Socialism

"If Socialism has to become a definite reality, then we must recognize that the problem of social reform is fundamental and that for them there is no escape from it. Unless Socialists do so, they cannot achieve their revolution."

Industrialization and State Socialism

"State Socialism is essential to the rapid industrialization of India. The private enterprise cannot do it."

****

2

My India

"For me, what else can be greater than India? This is my country; and this is the country of my brothers and sisters."

Superiority of Nation

"All [my] countrymen will learn that the country is greater than any individual."

Supremacy of Country

"I consider the nation greater than any individual whosoever great he may be. I am a greater nationalist than any other individual."

Indianness Supreme

"I do not like what some people say, that we are Hindus first or Muslim first and Indians afterwards. I frankly say that I do not want our loyalty as Indians should be in the slightest way affected by any competitive loyalty whether that loyalty arises out of our religion."

Indian First

"I want all people to be Indian first, Indian last and nothing else but Indian..."

Base of Progress

"A broad, mature and firm approach can be the basis of progress of the county in which the feeling of progress of the down-trodden people of the society is attached."

Devotion to Nation

"I love India very much; that is the true faith of a nationalist."

National Interest

"Whenever there has been a conflict between my personal interests and the interests of the country as a whole, I have always placed the country above my own personal claims."

National Approach

"Even while working to end an evil, a [broad] national approach must be there in mind."

Common Nationality

"I am of the opinion that the most vital need of the day is to create among the masses of the people the sense of a common nationality the feeling that they are Indian first and Hindus, Mohamedans or Sindhis, Kanarese afterwards...Nothing should be done which will harden local patriotism and group consciousness."

Service to Nation

"If I have rendered any service for the benefit of this country which may be considered to be patriotic one, I have rendered that service only due to my inner conscience."

****

3

Importance of Village

"The importance and state of villages will still alive for a long time. Therefore, the work in direction of social-equality has to be carried on for the village –level. It is also for this reason because the roots of the present system are present there."

Common Life

"Everybody is attached to the common-life; and because every change leaves impression upon everyone, therefore, each and everyone should get the right to decide his [own] terms..."

Village-Cleanliness

"It is not the responsibility of the few to make the village clean so that they may be fit for maintaining health and become ideal to provide equal opportunities to poor in general and Dalits in particular for their welfare and progress. For this task collective efforts are necessary, and it is also essential that the Government provide desired assistance in this task."

Village and Untouchability

"India is a land of villages and so long as the village system provides an easy method of marching out and identifying the Untouchables; the Untouchable has no escape from Untouchability."

****

Characteristics of Federal Constitution

"One of the characteristics of a Federal Constitution is that although the territory comprised in the Federal is distributed or held by different units, still they constitute one single territory."

Acid-Test of Constitution

"A Constitution, like a suit must fit. A Constitution which does not fit is no Constitution; it cannot be a Constitution."

Acceptance of Constitution

"If the Constitution is imposed and [it] is accepted by one section and is opposed by another, there will arise in the country an element, hostile to the Constitution, and which will devote its energies not to working the Constitution but to breaking it."

Protection of Constitution

"It is the co-operation that has accorded some such guarantees which were not possible by any other means."

Future Constitution

"The Constitution must be so made that it will not only command the obedience but also the respect of all; and all or if not all, at any rate, all important elements in the national life of India shall be prepared to uphold it and to give it their support."

****

5

Responsibility of Executive

"It is evident that the responsibility of the Executive would be of very little consequence if the Provincial Executive instead of being subordinate to the Provincial Legislature a subordinate to say other body outside the Province or if the Provincial Legislature instead of being supreme within its field is made subject to some other authority in the matter of the exercise of its power. In other words, to render Provincial Government autonomous, it is necessary to democrat clearly the sphere of operation of the Provincial and Central Governments."

Rights of Legislature

"The expediency of allowing a Legislature every power reasonably necessary to the existence of such a body and the proper exercise of the functions which it is intended to execute..."

Elected House

"Any ...House, howsoever dominated by the Executive, will not tolerate the candidature of any member of the House for office unless he shows that he has some power of speech, some dexterity in the handling of a subject, some readiness of reply and above all some definite vision which can constitute the basis of a rational policy of social and economic betterment."

Legislative Council

"I do not think that the arithmetic theory of representation can be agreed to. If the Legislative Council was a zoo or a museum wherein a certain number of each species was to be kept, such a theory of minority representation would have been tolerate."

Twofold Rule

"A return to a system, as the Dyarchy, which has been criticized, at this stage in the evolution of political life in India, is unthinkable."

Dyarchy

"The continuance of Dyarchy for an indefinite period, only because it has been successfully worked in the past, and [perhaps] it will work in future too, this assumption is quite untenable."

Impracticable System

"The Dyarchy is in itself an unworkable system of government."

Fall of Dualism

"The Dualism due to division of subjects is but one of the inherent defects which makes Dyarchy unworkable."

Criticism-Free Rule

"Of course Dyarchy with complete Dualism involving the functioning of two separate governments and separate legislatures, is free from the criticism which has been urged above against the system of Dyarchy-with-Dualism such is in operation"

Lawful System

"A system which enslaves the whole population, which smothers the spirit of progress, which blocks the way for furtherance, is a system which, I think no right-minded person, no man with any feelings, will sustain or will justify."

****

6

Nature of Law

"As far as possible the nature of the law should be non-violent and it should become violent only according to need."

Equality Before Law

"Equality before law is a valuable thing, but all men do not consider it to be valuable only for the one reason. Most of the people realize it as an ideal; and only few realize its complication. Equality before law compels the people to make it an issue of common concern with those who have equally affected by it."

Importance of Law and Order

"Law and order is the medicine of the body politic and when the body politic goes sick this medicine must be administered."

Taking of Law

"The failure to administer, it must be deemed to be crime against society and civilization"

Freedom of Man

"As the use of individual capabilities for the Government is most important, it is in the public interest to make it certain that one is not deprived of the opportunity of taking active part in the process of the Government."

Individual Freedom

"Men are born free and till death they hold the same position."

Secrete of Freedom

"You must abolish your slavery yourselves; do not depend for its abolition upon…anyone."

Fight for Freedom

"Will [any] other one make efforts to by heart to bring the end to our slavery? It you say "Yes", then I will ask you, "By which limit?" and "How?" Therefore, self-struggle for one's own freedom is the best way; and if someone achieves his freedom by self-sacrifice, then there is no alternative it. "

****

7

Significance of Government

"If today we are on the way to building a common nation, a spirit of nationality, a feeling that we are all one, it is due to the fact that we have a common Government; it is due to the fact that we realize that we are citizen of a common Government."

Public Government

"It is undeniable that a party is an essential adjunct to popular Government. [But] it is equally undeniable that the rule of a single party is fatal to popular Government."

Meaningful Government

"No Government worthy of its name, no Government with any sincerity can tell the poor classes that it cannot provide these amenities because it has not the courage to levy taxes.

Two-Party System

"Two party system is the safe system [in Democracy]. There should be a party [in opposition] to make critical analysis of the Government in the absence of which a Government can easily assume the form of Despotism."

Representative Government

"If the meaning of franchise is well-understood, it is the requirement of the appropriateness of a representative Government that its level should not be such that the majority of poor and ***Dalit*** Communities are not benefited by it."

Useless Government

"A Government that cannot accord facilities to poor should withdraw from the office as early as possible as it is good for all."

Popular Government

"The popular Government is not only Government for the people but by the people..."

Rule and Government

"...There must always be a Government to govern...It is of the highest value for the peace and tranquility of the people. For, when Constitutional Government fails, the breakdown clause has at least the merit of maintaining Government."

Condition of Popular Government

"The representation of opinion by itself is not sufficient to constitute a popular Government. To cover its true meaning it requires individual representation as well."

Government and Safety

"In steed of remaining out of the Government if I stay there, I can serve more for the interests of Scheduled Castes."

For Good Governance

"For the well-management of the Government [it is necessary that] the evils which take place there are rooted out."

Strong Government

"The Government, which can speak and act as per the wish of the people and unify the whole nation, is no doubt the strongest Government."

Government in Emergency

"Only a strong Government can be depended upon to act in an emergency."

Duty of Government

"Only a strong Government as a whole is to preserve peace and order, to protect the weak against the strong, and to see that in the disposal of all questions coming before them the conflicting interests of the many different classes affected receive due attention."

Accountability of Institution

"Government is an institution of accountability; it is dependent on public opinion."

Responsibility of Government

"One of the chief responsibilities of the Government is to carry out the solution to poverty. The Government should adopt such measures that the most of the people enjoy those facilities that are necessary to be called civilized."

Duty of Government

"If the Government desires that...people should work for them, it is absolutely necessary that Government should take upon its shoulders the responsibility of paying them."

Expectation of Government

"Our Government should be such in which the people in power could use all their energies in the best possible manner in the [general] interest of country. Our Government must be such that the people in power could work for the establishment of social and economic justice where [people have come forward to] resist with disobedience."

Central Government

"My conception of the position of the Central Government will not permit me to reconcile myself even to such a form of relationship as is found in the American Constitution in which the Central Government is a Commonwealth as well as a Union of Commonwealths."

Central Government of America

"The Central Government in the United States is a creature of the States. Having been called into existence by the States it must stand or fall with the States."

Criticism of Government

"No Government should be free from criticism."

****

8

Party Organization

"The reason behind failure of a [political party] is the lack of its organization."

Unorganized Party

"No [political] party has the right to be called itself a party if it is incapable to organize [the people]."

Affiliation With Political Party

"There is no gain if someone joins a political party merely as its follower."

Party and Government

"A party is necessary to run Government, but two parties are necessary to keep Government from being despotism.

Single Party System

"To have popular Government run by a single party is mere form for despotism to play its part from behind it."

Double Party System

"A democratic Government can remain democratic only if it is worked by two parties-a party in power and a party in opposition."

Party-Work

"Theoretically, political parties are agencies for the expression and execution of public opinion, but in practice parties create, direct, influence and often control public opinion."

Reality of Majority

"Those who depend upon the rule of majority, they, generally, forget the kind of reality of majority."

****

9

Significance of Democracy

"Democracy is essential as a governing principle of human relationship. Therefore, it is our duty to see that Democracy does not vanish from the face of the Earth."

Democratic Civilization

"It is necessary to maintain the basis of democratic civilization; if Democracy dies, it will be a doom."

Political Democracy

"Unless we all accept majority rule as the fundamental working principle, there can be no political democracy."

Ignorant Democracy

"The fate of ignorant democracy which refuses to follow the way shown by learning and experience and choose to grope in the dark paths of the mystics and the megalomaniacs is a said thing to contemplate."

Sacrifice in Democracy

"It is not correct to say that there is no need of sacrifice in establishing a Democracy. [In fact] in the establishment of a Democracy comparatively we need much more sacrifices."

Democracy and Political Party

"In a Democracy a political party is important, but it must have an able leader, programme and commitment to discipline, otherwise it cannot succeed."

Majority and Democracy

"No matter if the principle of majority is the basis of practices of Democracy, and no matter if it is considered the best and effective system of governance in the world, but this system too is not free from evils."

Reality of Majority

"It is a majority which is always made, unmade and remade."

Political Majority

"A political majority is not a fixed or a permanent majority."

Communal Majority

"A communal majority is a permanent majority fixed in its attitude."

****

10

Value of Franchise

"The poorer the individual, the greater the necessity of enfranchising him..."

Common Life and Franchise

"I do not think of any other meaning of franchise except of deciding terms for a common-life."

Arrangement of Franchise

"The franchise stands for direct and participation in the regulation of the term upon which associated life shall be sustained and the permit of good carried on..."

Democracy and Separate Elections

"There should be no provision for separate constituencies when a plan to implement the Democratic system in India is made."

Adult Franchise

"Adult suffrage, which is supported by political justice and founded by political expedience, is also demanded by a substantial body of public opinion."

Adult Franchise System

"In reality the adult franchise is the only arrangement that can be in consonance to its [word] meaning."

Getting Right to Vote

"On the strength of my conscious I have struggling for human rights of my people, and while doing so, I have never thought of causing any kind of loss to the nation."

Equal Right

"It is your birthright to get food, shelter and clothing in this land, and that too in equal proportion."

Struggle for Rights

"Taking it to be their duty many great men have sacrificed their lives for the protection of human rights. Even before entering in the young age it is much better to die for a great cause instead of doing nothing like a yoke."

Extensive Franchise

"Indeed we regard the development of a broad franchise as the arch on which the edifice of self-government must be raised: for we have no intention that our reforms should result merely in the transfer of power from a bureaucracy to an oligarchy."

Sense of Separate Election

"The landlords, the capitalists, and the priests have an immense influence in every society, but no one has ever conceded that these classes should be given an immense share of representation. There is, therefore, no reason why the Mohamedan claim should be recognized when claims of similar nature have been dismissed elsewhere.

Harm of Separate Election

"I am against the [Muslim] representation through separate electorates. Territorial electorates and separate electorates are two extremes which must be avoided."

Separate Elections and Muslims

"India is not the only country where Mohamedans are not in a majority. There are other countries in which they occupy the same position. But the Mohamedan Communities not insisted there upon the necessity of separate communal electorates. As all students of political history are aware the Mohamedans in these countries have managed without the benefit of separate electorates..."

Counter Claim of Separate Elections

"The Mohamedan's is not the only case of a ruling class which has suffered a fall in its position. The French in Canada and the Dutch in South Africa are the other instances where a class fell from its position of a ruling class to that of a subject class. But neither the French in Canada nor the Dutch in South Africa put forth claims to extravagant representation in order to be able to maintain their former position as rulers, nor is such a consideration shown to Mohamedan minorities in other parts of the world. The Mohamedan minorities in Albania, Romania, Greece and Bulgaria are the remnants of what was once a ruling race. Yet in none of these countries have they claimed a royal share of representation. The Mohamedan claim for representation according to the influence is not only, not heard of, but is quite foreign to the system of representative government."

****

11

Fundamental of Politics

"Politics is nothing if it is not realistic. There is very little in it that is academic. It is therefore followed that before passing any judgments on any scheme of politics, it is essential that one must consider the ground plan."

Political Structure

"The political structure depends upon social structure...The social structure leaves a deep impression upon political structure."

Politics and National Leadership

"The politics is not my first love nor is national leadership the goal of my life."

Panchasheela in Politics

"Firstly there is no room for Panchasheela in politics; and secondly, not in politics of the Communist country. The Communist countries have two well-known principles on which they always act. One of them is that morality is always in a flux; there is no morality. Today's morality is not tomorrow's morality. Asia has been the cockpit of war.

More than half of Asia is Communist. It has adopted a different principle of life and a different principle of government. It is therefore better to align ourselves with what we call free nations if we believe in freedom"

Statesman

"A politician acts not only of politics, but he represents a particular belief in which both-the practices and principles of politics-are included."

Rightness of Political Gain

"When a [particular] community becomes strong and asks for some political benefits, then some concessions are given to it so that its good–will could be obtained. But [doing so], neither a proper inquiry of its claims is made, nor a decision on the basis of involved virtues [or vices] is taken [in the matter]. Consequently, such claims or concessions become limitless."

****

12

Dictatorship

"Even to make despotism the subject to election is no guarantee against it. The real guarantee against despotism is to confront it with the possibility of its dethronement."

Dictator

"A Dictator might, as the king did in the olden times, put out one by one the teeth of a few without necessarily exciting the resentment of the other people."

Dictatorship and Freedom

"Despotism is antithetical of freedom whether the despotism is native or foreign."

Dictatorship v/s Freedom

"Those who believe in individual freedom strongly object to Dictatorship and insist upon Parliamentary Democracy as a proper form of government for a free society. For, they feel that freedom of an individual is possible only under Parliamentary Democracy and not under Dictatorship."

****

13

Teacher and Student

"The pupil only takes his guidance from his master. He is not bound to accept his master's conclusions. There is no ingratitude in the disciple not accepting maxims or the conclusion of his master."

True Education

"In true kind of education a student learns to make difference between thought and reality. He must be able to make distinction among the basic issues and should be capable to understand every question on the basis of virtue without the support of any principle in vogue.

Education and Existence

"Without education, the existence is not safe..."

A True Teacher

"Only he can be a true teacher who himself has been honest in his studies. One who himself has never been honest in the process of study and who is not neutral in approach, he cannot be expected of honesty and neutrality in his teaching work."

Qualifications of a Teacher

"Who should be a teacher? What should be the qualifications of a teacher? These are the questions in discussion since the olden times and the outcome of them has ultimately become the basis for the appointment of a teacher, however, it is another matter that this self-existent basis of the outcome has been sound or not!"

Importance of Teacher

"The class of teacher occupies an important place in the life of the country. Therefore, it is necessary that this class should be selected with extra care. It is also important because the important work of social reform is carried out by teachers. In such a situation, if teachers are of narrow mentality and not of sound mentality, they cannot be able to work in right direction of social work."

Ambitious Educationist

"It is necessary to prevent adventurous educationists from opening individual autonomous colleges in all sorts of unseemly and unpromising towns."

Teacher and Dependence

"A professor who is made to work in that gallery slave fashion can never be a teacher in the real sense of the world. He can only be a hack doing a task with the help of ready-made notes. We cannot expect originality from him and he can give no inspiration to those who may have the misfortune to listen to him. The whole study bound to be a merely mechanical process..."

Gain from Education

"No doubt, education is the greatest material benefit."

Advantageous Education

"If there is a desire to make education beneficial and real then such kind of efforts be made that it does not remain limited to the rich people. It is essential that education be cheap so that it could be available to poor."

Control-Free Education

"To bring the real progress in the field of education, it is necessary to make it free from the control of handful individuals, or a particular group of individuals.

Original Student

"Instead of becoming an original student of University, a studying person should come upon the perceptive vision of those situations for which original research is being carried out. A student should be capable of identifying the realities. He should follow them and should establish morality on the basis of sound deliberation."

Duty of Student

"It is the duty of student to know carefully about those things whose conclusions have been forcibly denied by him. He should possess the capability of investigating the things said earlier; he should also be capable of estimating the result before accepting or rejecting the thing."

Scholarship

"My experiences show that the method of giving scholarship is really a waste of public money."

Reality of Scholarship

"The depressed class parents are too poor, too ignorant; to understand that the help given by Government is really the help for the education of the child. The scholarship is looked upon by the parent as the family aid to meet their expenses. It is certainly not made available for the education of the boy as such, which is the primary object of scholarship."

Scholarship and Goal

"With the scholarship, I have found that the boy is never able to reach the goal."

University-Education

"The aim and functions of university education should be to see that the teaching carried on there is suited to adults; that it is scientific, detached and impartial in character; that it aims not so much at filling the mind of the student with fact or theories as at calling forth his own individuality and stimulating him to mental effort; that it accustoms him to critical study of the leading authorities, with perhaps, occasional reference to first hand sources of information, and that it implants in his mind a standard of thoroughness, and gives him a sense of the difficulty as well as the value of reaching at truth."

Existence of University

"I do no think that any university in any civilized country can justify its existence if it merely deals with the problems of examinations and the granting of degrees."

A Complete University

"The university should have the Faculties of Engineering, Agriculture, Fine Arts, Technology and Music to make it a complete university."

Basic Work of University

"One of the fundamental work functions of the university is to provide facilities for bringing the highest education to the doors of the needy and the poor."

Work of University

"The universities cannot [merely] be sown broadcast."

Right of University

"As a matter of fact, the university has no power to amend the ways of the colleges."

University and Library

"No university can function without a first rate library attached to it."

Management of University

"Before a university can be in a position to fulfill the aims and functions of university education, it must be so organized that it becomes essentially a place of learning, where a corporation scholars labour in comradeship for the training of men and the advancement and diffusion of knowledge."

Level of University

"A great deal depends upon what kind of "stuff' the university gets from the high schools. How to get the right kind of stuff is a problem with every university."

Success of University

"For a university, to succeed, it is necessary to group together certain branches of knowledge which students pursue."

Goal of University

"The university cannot succeed in promoting research or in promoting higher education, if it makes the examination system the beginning and end to its existence."

Character of University

"The university should be a centralized institution and if the plans of a new university were to be laid down ***ab intigro***, it would be better to rule out the type in which a university was to be composed of affiliated colleges."

****

Position of Governor

"Such a position for a Governor which makes him to play the double role of an autocrat and a constitutional head is not a very happy position."

Power of Governor

"What is necessary for making the Governor a constitutional head, is to take away his power of certification and suspension."

Disassociation of Governor

"The Governor should not be a part of the executive nor shall he have the right to preside over it."

Life of Minister

"Ministers of the country, who are the first citizens of the country, should lead a life that is cultured, that cares for arts, that cares for learning, and that ought to be a model for the rest."

Salary of Minister

"There are four considerations which ought to prevail while deciding of the salary of a minister: social standard of the ministers; consideration of competency;

consideration of democracy; and consideration of integrity and purity of administration."

Position of Minister

"A minister is a subject to the vagaries of public opinion and likely to be swayed by communal prejudices."

****

15

Expectation of Justice

"A population which is hidebound by caste, a population which is infected by ancient prejudices, a population which flouts equality of states and is dominated by notions of gradation in life, a population which thinks that some are high, that some are low-can it be expected to have the right notions even to discharge bare justice?"

Sacrifice for Justice

"[Along with justices] if someone desires to enjoy rights, he should struggle for them by heart and soul and if necessary be ready even to sacrifice his life..."

Proper Equality

"Those who believe in lawful equality, they accept the reality of taking on the people living below poverty line, and they make sincere efforts in direction of their social-economic equality. Unless there is no equality of status, no equality can be established in reality. In fact, equality means equality at all levels and not at some of the levels."

Equality

"Now, equality should become the fundamental principle; the policy of deciding opportunities on the basis of low and high should come to an end."

Equal Right

"Equality in getting food, clothing and house is your fundamental right."

Characteristics of Judiciary

"A judiciary before it could be entrusted must have three requisites: first of all, it must be trained in law; then it must be impartial in outlook; and it must be independent in position."

Judge and Justice

"We, not only want justice, but we want judges who are competent to discharge their duties."

****

16

Life Philosophy

"Every man should have a philosophy of life; for, everyone must have a standard by which to measure his conduct, and to maintain it; philosophy of life is nothing, but a standard by which to measure..."

Elements of Good Life

"The feeling of unity, a system based on equality before law and equal treatment by the administrative body- these are the fundamentals for a meaningful life."

Life of Action

"Certainly, for the fulfillment of necessary wants of a practical life, we give priority to one of them, but while doing so, we should be careful so that other ones are not sacrificed."

Meaningful Life

"Life can be ennobled and immortalized by sacrificing it for a lasting good such as the cause of truth, vow, honour or country.

Dependent Life

"Dragging on life somehow or to live a crow for a thousand years is not the only and worthy way to live in this world."

Basis of Social Philosophy

"Positively, my social philosophy may be said to be enshrined in three words: liberty, equality and fraternity; I have not borrowed it from anywhere. My philosophy has roots in religion and not in political science. I have derived them from the teachings of my master, the [Great] Buddha."

A True Intellectual

"No one with narrowness can be a true intellectual; one who tries to gain for individual ends; he is not a true intellectual."

Intellectual Community

"The intellectual class is the class which can foresee; it is the class which can advice and can give lead. In no country does the mass of people live the life of intelligent thought and action. It is largely imitative and follows the intellectual class. There is no exaggeration in saying that the entire destiny of a country depends upon its intellectual class. If the intellectual class is honest, independent and disinterested it can be trusted to take the initiative and give a proper lead when a crisis arises. It is true that intellect by itself is no virtue. It is only a means and the use of means depends upon the ends which an intellectual person pursues. An intellectual man can be a good man but he can easily be a rogue. Similarly an intellectual class may be a bend of high-soul person, ready to help, ready to emancipate erring humanity..."

****

17

For Proper Deed

"It is better to act even violently as in war than not at all for only when we act that we may hope to act well."

Significance of Deed

"The importance of the principle of the *Karma* cannot be denied in any circumstances. Without the *Karma* life will become aimless. Therefore, I have always been in favour of *Karmas* and in a message to my [own] people I have conveyed them never to withdraw themselves from [the process of] the *Karmas*."

Great Man

"A great man must be motivated by the dynamics of a social purpose and must act as the scourge and the scavenger of society."

Identity of Great Man

"No great man really does his work by crippling his disciples by forcing on them his maxims or his conclusions. What a great man does is not to impose his maxims on his disciples. What he does is to evoke them, to awaken them to a vigorous and various exertions of their faculties."

Repentances of Great Man

"Posterity is always interested in the last words and last regrets of great men, but their regrets are always significant and worth pondering over."

****

Perception of Co-operation

"I do not believe in the theory of opposing only to oppose...Where something can be gained by co-operation there we should have the feeling of co-operation."

Compromise for Good

"If I have compromise with those who have different plans or the way of working than me, or if I have liked to work with them, I have done so only to accord something good to my [own] people and to strengthen, more or less, my mission."

Compromise with Wishful

"As one who believes in the necessity of knowledge and appreciates the difficulties in its acquisition, I am glad to be associated in this way with him."

Oneness

"Unity is possible only through that equal devotion which occurs on the basis of common legislation..."

Communal Harmony

"If all communities have to be accorded equal status then it is possible only through a sympathetic behaviour with those who are living below the level."

Dream of Unity

"No one will be able to obstruct India's unity and one day all our Castes and Classes shall work with unity."

Secret of Unity

"If we want to build up unity, what we should do is to break up the social barrier...In this matter the lead has to be taken up by Hindu Community."

Progress Through Unity

"Without the help of those who are deprived of means and Dalits today, no progress for India can be imagined."

Solution Through Co-operation

"A system cannot become delightful unless the others extend their co-operation. In case of struggle between two communities, the permanent remedy is possible only going in the root cause of that struggle. In this regard it is also essential that there must be honesty and impartiality in course of process of [getting a] solution to the problem."

Gain By Co-operation

"As far as the possibility of gain through co-operation is there, why is there need to oppose? Why not is the thing be obtained through co-operation if a possibility to do so remain there?"

Struggle With Unity

"Go ahead with unity; you will get power and honour on the basis of [your own] struggle."

Future Unity

"Today we are divided politically, socially and economically, but this situation will not remain for ever. No doubt, in future we will come forward with unity."

Brotherhood

"The foundation of a State is laid upon fraternity. What is this fraternity or sympathy? In brief, it is the outcome of collective feeling of unity of those who realize that they all are brothers."

****

19

Language and Unity

"While accepting the principle of linguistic province, it must provide against the break up of India's unity."

Linguistic Province

"While accepting the demand for the re-constitution of province on linguistic basis, the Constitution should provide that the official language of every province is the same as the official language of the Central Government [of India]."

Meaning of Linguistic Province

"By a linguistic province, I mean a province which by social composition of its population is homogeneous."

Province in the Name of Language

"The formation of a province merely in the name of language is not a practical aspect of the principle. A province should be created with the point of view of capability, availability of good administration and possibility of maximum welfare of the people. Sound and good administration, maximum possible diminution in people's difficulties and ardent development should be the criteria of creating a province."

Principle of Linguistic Province

"The principle of one language one province is too large to be given effect to in practice. The number of provinces that will have to be carved out it the principle is to be carried out to its logical conclusion."

Bilingual Province

"Bilingual provinces due to their advantageous state should be retained."

Opportunities in Bilingual Province

"In a bilingual province people get equal opportunities for participation; therefore, I believe that it controls the tendencies of separatism on a large scale."

Communal Base of Province

"When the communal feeling is running at full tide and the national feeling is running at low, would there be time for creating provinces on the basis of [religious] community?"

****

20
Untouchable Man

"In the national sense Untouchable is a person who is deemed to belong to a class which is commonly held to cause pollution by touch; although contact with such a person may for local circumstances not be avoided or may not necessitate ceremonial purification."

Authority of Untouchability

"What makes the Untouchability so difficult, to break the system of Untouchability is the religious sanction which it has behind it."

Kind of Untouchability

"Among the Hindus [of India] the Untouchability is a notion of different kind, and the rest of the world is unknown to this kind of thing. In any other society, in any age-whether pre-historic, ancient or modern-no such thing is found. It is the outcome of intensive study and research."

Removal of Untouchability

"For the removal of Untouchability we have to start work from villages where it is deep rooted."

Untouchable and Untouchability

"It is wrong to say that the Untouchables were always Untouchables. We have to accept that in a state all, Untouchables or ancestors of all [others] were the same; and only on accepting this reality, the misleading and imaginary recognition of Untouchability can be rooted out."

Permanent Untouchability

"Dirty localities adjacent to villages make Untouchability permanent."

Nature of Caste

"If Caste is an attitude and it is nothing else, it must be asked to dissolve when that particular attitude symbolizing the Caste is dissolved."

Problem of Caste

"The Caste problem is a vast one, both, theoretically and practically."

Caste and Inequality

"The problem of Caste, then, ultimately resolves itself into one of repairing the disparity between the marriageable units of the two sexes within it."

Caste and Nation

"The Caste is a nation but the rule of one Caste over another may not be admitted to be the same as the rule of one nation over another."

Rule of Caste

"The Caste rule must mean the rule in terms of Caste interest and Caste prejudices."

Removal of Caste System

"Real method of breaking up the Caste System is not to bring about inter-Caste dinners and inter-Caste marriages, but to destroy the religious notions on which Caste was founded."

End of Caste-Feeling

"The existing set attitude representing the diverse Castes and groups will be dissolved only if the diverse groups meet together and take part in a common activity."

Problem of Caste System

"The Caste System has killed the spirit of the people. It has destroyed the sense of public charity. It is that system which has made impossible to reach a consensus."

Casteless Hindu Society

"When the Hindu Society becomes a Casteless Society then it can hope to have strength enough to defend itself."

Caste and Social Inability

"We possess in ourselves many desires and ambitions of that Caste or Community in which we are born, and [doping so] we feel inability of society."

Varna System and Untouchability

"One of the characteristics of the system of Untouchability and also of the Caste System is that the social status of the individual rises or falls with that of the community [*Varna*] to which he belongs."

Reality of Four Varnas

"This general opinion that the principle of social organization of the Indian ***Aryans***, which means the society is divided into four parts-***Brahmins*** [priests], ***Kshattriyas*** [soldiers], ***Vaishyas*** [traders] and ***Shudras*** [slaves], does not submit any solution to the problems of the ***Shudras***; nor does it indicate any importance of them. If the ***Chaturvarna*** means only the division of the Society into four parts, and nothing else, then it would be a very innocent principle. Unfortunately, there has been much more in its field, and it is the reality."

****

Reality of Dharma

"I say that religion is for man and not man for religion."

True Dharma

"The religion which discriminates between two followers is partial, and the religion which inflicts upon them insufferable disabilities is no religion at all. Religion and slavery are incompatible."

Acid Test of Dharma

"The religion that does not recognize you as human being is not worthy to be called a religion. The religion that forbids you to come in the way of advancement is not a religion."

Necessity of Dharma

"Some people think that religion is not essential to society. I do not hold this view. I consider the foundation of religion to be essential to life and practices of society."

Dharma-Adharma

"The ***Dharma*** that compels the ignorant to be ignorant and poor to be poor is not the ***Dharma***..."

Real Dharma

"I agree with Burke that a true religion is the foundation of society on which all Citizen Governments depend."

Reform in Dharma

"The religion is essential, but I hold that reform in religion, too, is a necessary aspect."

****

22

Value of Agriculture

"In a country like India that depends almost wholly upon farming the importance of agriculture cannot be exaggerated."

Vices of Agriculture

"Our bad social economy is responsible for the ill of our agriculture."

Agriculture and Industrialization

"If our agricultural-holdings are small and scattered, we can certainly propose a solution by the reflex effect of industrialization."

Small Holdings

"We must strongly hold that the evils of small holdings in India are not fundamental but are derived from the parent evil of the mal-adjustment in her social economy. Consequently, if we wish to affect a permanent cure we must go to the parent malady."

Reduction in Land Revenue

"I take the liberty of saying that the land revenue should be reduced; I am for it and I will insist upon it because I say that the Government has really no right to take what are called profits of agriculture."

Profitable Holding

"By fixing the size of a holding [an economist] can only make it a large holding, but not an economic holding. For, an economic holding is not a matter of size of land alone, but it is a matter of the adjustment of a piece of land to the necessary equipment for its efficient cultivation."

Desire of Profitable Holding

"It is desired by all interested in our agriculture that our holdings should be economic holdings."

Size of Holdings

"The size of the holding should be such that when necessary it could be transformed in a profitable manner and on the basis of production."

Legal State of Holding

"He would be a poor economist who would legally fix the size of the holding which in the interest of economic production must be left to vary when variation is demanded."

Solution of Profitable Holding

"The diminutive size of holdings is said to be greatly harmful to Indian Agriculture. The evils of small holdings, no doubt, are many. But it would have been no slight mitigation of them if the small holdings were compact holdings."

Land Reform

"We need a comprehensive and long-termed plan to reform our agriculture sector; side-by-side, comparatively we need to do something concrete in this regard."

Agricultural System

"In India, crores of people, or in other words most of the population, depends upon farming. Also in many years to come its importance will not be exaggerated. Therefore, we utterly need of some such reforms in the agriculture sector that could prove to be profitable; they could be advantageous to both-the farmers and their co-workers."

Agricultural Equipments

"What is the use of enlarging the farms if the farmer has not got wherewithal to cultivate the land."

Population of Cultivators

"In India a large agricultural population with the lowest proportion of land in actual cultivation means that a large part of agricultural population is superfluous and idle."

Agricultural Reform

"The remedy for the ills of agriculture in India does not lie primarily in the matter of enlarging holdings, but in the matter of increasing capital and capital goods."

Condition of Chakabandi

"The Industrialization at lager scale is important to facilitate to ***Chakabandi*** [consolidation]

Success of Chakabandi

"It should never be forgotten that unless we have constructed an effective barrier against the future sub-division and fragmentation of a consolidated holding, it is idle to lay out plans for ***Chakabandi*** [consolidation]. Such a barrier can only be found industrialization; for, it alone can reduce the extreme pressure, as we have shown, causes sub-division of land."

****

23

Labourer and Social Justice

"Placing the principle of social justice above all, working hours should be made the part of duty of workers and there should not be slightest trace of recognition to workers' exploitation, and by doing so, [definitely] the [industrial] disputes can be resolved."

Idle Labour

"The depression of our national dividend is another important effect of idle labour."

Meaning of Strike

"In plain popular language, a strike is nothing more than a breach of contract of service. When a worker strikes, all that it means is that he commits a breach of contract of service: there is more in it, and nothing less to it."

Right to Strike

"The right to strike is simply another name for the right to freedom."

Divine Right

"If you accept the right to freedom is a divine right, then I contend that the right to strike is a divine right."

Strike and Patience

"In regard to strike, if a step is taken in haste, it cannot bring any fruit."

Ban on Strike

"If you want to restrict the right to strike and want to make it illegal, then you must do it only in relation to service on which the sustenance of the life of community depends."

Action Against Labour

"If the breach of peace is caused by some unreasonable demand made by labour, you may be justified in using police force against them. On the other hand, if the peace is broken by something which has been done by the employer that does not stand to reason and which is contrary to justice and equality, the Government have no right to use the police force against workers."

Good Industrial System

"To make the industrial order delightful, three things are necessary: 1-Machinary; 2-Amendment in the Industrial [Commercial] Dispute Bill; and 3-To decide minimum daily wage in accordance with law."

Power and Industrial Peace

"No peace in the industrial sphere is possible through the use of power. It may be possible through legislation, but [even then] there is no guarantee that it gets certainty."

****

Communal Approach

"Everyone in India is bound to look at every question consciously or unconsciously from communal point of view."

Communal View

"I myself look at every question from a communal point of view and ask myself whether it would be good for the depressed classes or not."

Communal Representation

"I am totally opposed to the recognition of communal representation in the executive of the country. Under it the disease will break out in its worst form in a most vital organ of the Government machinery."

Unfortunate-Riots

"Disturbances are no doubt very unfortunate. But they could never be otherwise. The only question is this: whether in maintaining peace and order, we shall not have regard for freedom and liberty."

Cause of Riots

"An unlawful assembly becomes a riot when that assembly uses force. Thus the offence of rioting really arises out of an offence of unlawful assembly."

Spot on Society

"We have had very serious riots...which have been a disgrace to Indian Society and Indian Civilization, and, I am sure, one cannot dispute on this issue."

Unbearable Threat

"The spark fact that a Muslim, without caring for anything goes and stabs a Hindu, and a Hindu, without caring for anything, stabs a Mohamedan, is a calamity, which we could never tolerate."

Hindu-Muslim

"I do not think that Hindus and Mohamedans, constituted as they are, can honestly say that they are non-communal in their attitude towards each other."

Hindu-Muslim Reality

"There can be no gainsaying about this that every Hindu and every Mohamedan is born in certain Caste or a Community. There is no gainsaying that we are brought up and bread up in a communal environment."

Solution of Communalism

"The approach I am making for the solution of the communal problem is based upon two considerations:

"1-In proceeding to solve the communal problem, it is essential to define the governing principles which should be invoked for determining the final solution; and

"2-Whatever the governing principles they must be applied to all parties equally without fear or favour."

****

Meaning of Knowledge

"Merely ascertaining and adhering to ideas is not the knowledge. The knowledge is a process that makes our development firm and increases our creativity and activity."

Knowledge and Life

"Knowledge is the foundation of man's life and every effort must be made to maintain the intellectual stamina of a student and develop his intellect."

Thinker and Patience

"Before proposing any doctrine, [it is necessary for] the thinker to have [enough] patience; he should also make self-analysis of the doctrine. For the establishment of the doctrine the thinker should not make haste, nor should he propose the doctrine without proper verification."

Honesty and Argument

"I have no expectations from my critics; what I expect of them is that they should present their case honestly and logically. There is no honesty in criticism if it is recourse to criticize only."

Advantageous Search

"Without imagination [there is] no possibility of proper research. It is also a reality that where there is a keen desire to prove the imagination to be true, the imagination becomes the poison for Science there as Michel too has truly said, 'Imagination is the acid of Science'."

Means and Ends

"Ends and means [=force in operation] are concomitants and the common adage that the end justifies the means contains a profound truth which is perverted simply because it is misunderstood."

Rightness of Means-Ends

"If the end does not justify the means what else will...?"

Achievement of Goal

"Our difficulty is that we do not sufficiently control the operations of the means once employed for the achieving of some end."

Achieving Goal-Means

"[We should keep in mind], that for a means when once employed liberates many ends-a fact scarcely recognized and not the one only we wish it to produce. However, in our fanaticism for achievement we attach the article "the" to the end we cherish and pay no heed to the ends simultaneously liberated."

****

26

Soul of Democracy

"The soul of Democracy is the doctrine of one man, one vote."

Parliamentary Democracy

"Those who want freedom are not prepared to give up Parliamentary Democracy as a form of Government."

Constitution of Democracy

"The Constitution of Democracy should go beyond [the institutions of] adult franchise and fundamental rights."

Criticism in Democracy

"A Democracy that escapes from criticism cannot step towards maturity. If Democracy has to become mature, if it has to function as per the expectation of the people, then it should accord the provision to a healthy criticism. Any situation opposite to it cannot make the Democracy a real one, and I cannot extend support to such a nominal Democracy."

Real Citizenship

"The most destructive is the theology of true Citizenship."

Significance of Citizenship

"The right of representation and the right to hold office under the State are the two most important rights that make up Citizenship."

****

27

Construction of Temple

"The temples have been built for the benefit of the followers of Hinduism, and this is the reason that they belong to all Hindus; they must be open to the Untouchable [Hindus] for the simple reason even if they are not built with their aid."

Use of Temple

"Some of the temples are private property, but [even then] they are for the use of all Hindus; and since the Untouchables are too called Hindus, they are entitled to enter into the temples to worship deity."

Necessity of Hinduism

"[It is necessary] for Hinduism to become a religion based on social equality, only then it will get recognition as a religion of nationalists."

Hindutva

"***Hindutva*** belongs as much to Untouchables as to the Touchable Hindus."

****

Secret of Courage

"Freedom is the secret of courage and the courage is born when people come together in a party."

Slave Mentality

"A slave cannot expect freedom unless he does not give up his slave-mentality."

New Life and Renaissance

"It is better to die and relieve this world if you cannot rise to a new life and if you cannot rejuvenate yourselves."

Self-Respect and Progress

"No community can rise at the cost of its self-respect. Therefore, if you...want to rise you must be treated as free citizens in society; you must be accorded opportunity to rise freely."

Respectful Life

"If you believe in living a respectful life, you believe in self-help that is the best help."

Self-Respect in Life

"We are valiant; we are not slaves. No other life is worst than a life without the feeling of nationalism and self-respect."

Life of Self-Respect

"Impermanent is the life of man. One day he has to die. Therefore, it must be decided [by all of us] that we will give up our life by fulfilling the efforts in the direction of making the life meaningful and achieving the ideal of self-respect."

True Interest

"Who other knows our interest better than us? For it we cannot permit anybody else no matter how big he is. Our interest is ours and we ourselves will reveal it."

Golden Future

"Those who are unable to defend themselves today one day they will become strong and because justice exists on Earth no one will be able to retain the same situation in which people's life is full of grievances. On the other hand the acid test of India's progress can be found in fact that what it has done for those who live the life full of difficulties and grievances."

Discrimination and National Loss

"The policy of discrimination has not only affected the Untouchables, but it has ultimately damaged the dignity of the nation and society."

Propagation of Views

"The life of man is destructive and the same rule applies to thoughts. It is wrong to say that thoughts can propagate themselves. As plants need water, in the same manner, thoughts need propagation. Otherwise both will fade."

Abandoned Views

"We should give up those views in which it has been said that parents give birth to the child and they are not Lord of his destiny. In fact, they can make his future."

Transitory Life

"Leave useless conversations and do not put your life on stake for me. Who can stop my death? Therefore, anything that can cause harm to your life, do not indulge in that at all for me."

Secret of Progress

"A society keen to keep a person on the level of God goes on the path of destruction. No one possesses extra virtues; one who makes progress, he achieves it by his own efforts."

Cultural Harmony of India

"There is no country that can rival the Indian peninsula with respect to the unity of its culture. It has not only a geographic unity, but it has over and above all a deeper and much more fundamental unity-the indubitable cultural unity that covers the land from end-to-end."

Importance of Man

"From time immemorial man as compared with woman has had the upper hand. He is dominant figure in every group and of the two sexes has the greater prestige. With this traditional superiority of man over woman his wishes have always been consulted."

Social-Political Structure

"It is our duty to take courageous steps and through our Constitution define both – economic and political structure [of India]."

Self-Defence of Motherland

"Do not be under the false impression that Pakistan would be able to spread its Muslim empire over India. We, ourselves, will defend our land."

Defence of Motherland

"I confess I have my quarrel with the Caste Hindus over some points, but I take a vow before you that I shall lay down my life in defence of our land."

****

Reality of Kashmir

"If we cannot save the whole of Kashmir, at least let us save our kith and kin; it is a plain analysis of the fact, which cannot be denied."

Problem of Kashmir

"The right solution of Kashmir issue is to partition of the State. Give the Hindu and Buddhist parts to India and Muslim part to Pakistan."

Kashmir-Policy

"I do not agree to the policy adopted by the Government of India regarding Kashmir, because it is not a political one."

Movement of League

"I have no hesitation in saying that, notwithstanding the agitation of the [Muslim] League for the partition of India, some day enough light will dawn upon the Muslims themselves, and they, too, will begin to think that a United India is better for everybody."

Intention of Jinnah

"If Jinnah is in favour of Muslim majority in Muslim Provinces, why he is opposed to a Hindu majority in the

Centre? Jinnah's position is in consistent. He cannot be expected to the affirmation of the principle of majority rule."

Foreign Policy

"The keynote of our foreign policy is to solve the problems of other countries and not to solve the problems of our own country."

End of War

"War cannot be abolished by merely refusing to fight when attacked. To abolish war, you must win war and establish a just peace."

Economic Plan

"A study of economic practices of the way of life is always important."

Principle of Economics

"One of the universal principles of economics is this that the capital is gained from the savings and the savings are possible if we have [too] much crops."

Economic Power

"The economic power is the only kind of power, no student of human society can accept..."

Source of Income

"Like an individual the income of society too depends upon currently available goods and the efforts made in this direction."

Social Capital

"What society has [in the name of capital], that depends upon available goods, or upon the last production."

Social Structure

"Those who want to raise the economic structure of society on the principle of the State Socialism; they must understand that through it they cannot base this fundamental achieving-purpose upon a simple law."

Price for Goods

"The good things of life do not fall from heaven like ***Mannat***; they have never done so anywhere. If fact, if you want the good things of life, you have got to pay for them. Unless you pay for them, you cannot get them."

Goods Gain

"I am one of those who believe in having the good things of life and also believe in having to pay for them."

****

Collective Responsibility

"To achieve through collective responsibility is an important thing."

True Parents

"There is no difference between parents and animals if they will not desire to see their children in a better position than their own."

Parent's Responsibility

"Your children follow you. Therefore, fulfil their life with virtues and qualities so that they can leave the significant signs of their identities in the world."

Inspiration of Children

"If you expect good and solid results from your children and if you also expect self dependence in them then you should inspire them to leap ahead on the basis of hard work and zeal."

Towards Unequal

"Equal treatment to the people who are unequal themselves is according to me simply another name for indifference and neglect."

Un-equality

"The principle of classification of human society on the basis of inequality is against the principle of nationalism."

Gaining of Right

"You cannot get your lost rights through begging; they cannot be acquired by prayer. If you want them, you would have to come forward to unvarying struggle."

Discerning Decision

"Be attentive! Do not jump in the fire just because I ask you to do so. Do it if you trust that you can get justice in it."

Way to Oppose

"Repulsion of crisis can be done by searching new methods. When you do not find a new way or method then the society gets diminished. Time [itself] provides an expected new way [to it] but it is Man who proceeds on the right track and not the time."

Backward Castes

"[In India] the position of Backward Classes is worse than that of Mohamedans and if the most favoured treatment is to be given to those who deserve it and the most then the

Backward Classes deserve more attention than do the Mohamedans."

Slavery

"In the root of slavery is the feeling that the slaves have no right except of those only that the ruling class accords them by its own wish."

Removal of Slavery

"If you want your slavery to be rooted out, and in a struggle to end the slavery if you face trails in courts, I will consider it to be a thing of pride and success; however the whole credit of it will go to you."

Self-Sufficiency

"We can become self-depend if we understand [the reality of] self-help; and only in such a situation we would be able to defend our self-respect except of gaining knowledge."

Self-Determination

"After all consideration if you come to the conclusion that you should struggle then go ahead firmly and without suspicion."

Branches of Knowledge

"Some of the branches of knowledge are deeply inter-related to each other, and where they are near enough to each other, they submit similarity in approaches..."

Our Mission

"Our mission must be to impart education equally to those brothers, sisters and daughters who are in our touch or who are near to us. For progress, education is absolutely necessary, none can deny its outcome, and we have to understand it."

Change

"Everything is changing; change is the law of life for individuals as well as for society."

Enemy of People

"A man who is bent upon breaking up such little industry, such little urbanization, as we possess is certainly no friend of the people...I take upon him as an enemy of the people."

Significance of Life

"I agree to the statement in which it has been said that, because everyman gets life only once, he must be accorded full opportunities to rise in the best possible manner."

Friendly Practice

"My relations with friend will always remain unchanged. Likewise, my conduct with the rest of the world will also remain unchanged. For friends, the doors of my house will never close."

Friend, not Enemy

"Many regard me as their enemy. But I have personal friends from even the ***Brahmin*** Community. Standing where I am, it has fallen to my lot to lash the anti-social actions of those who treat my people worse than dogs and cats impede their progress."

Protection of Community

"No community can become protector of other community even if the former is much superior to the later from intellectual point of view."

Reality of India

"India is not Europe; India is not England... Consequently, the political arrangement that may suit England cannot suit us. Let us recognize this fact."

Reservation

"Separate electorates or reservation of seats must not be restored to."

Minorities

"Minorities consist of those who lost their rights for the sins of their co-religionists."

Minority-Education and Level

"The power obviously depends upon the educational and economic status of minorities. The higher the education and economic status of minority the lesser is the need for that minority of being politically protected. On the other hand the lower the educational and economic status of minority, the greater will be the need for its political protection."

Chief Points of Buddhism

"There are four chief points of Buddhism:

"1-The society must have either the sanction of law or the sanction of morality to hold it together; without either the society is sure to go to pieces;

"2-Religion, if it is to function, must be in accord with reason, which is another name of science;

"3-It is not enough for religion to consist of a moral code, but its moral code must recognize the fundamental tenets of liberty, equality and fraternity; and

"4-Religion must not sanctify or ennoble poverty."

Unique Acid Test

"I do not forbid you if you consider a particular thing to be unique and different. But, why is it unique and what different is in it? You must know it. Merely on the basis of someone's statement or by listing a thing does not become unique or different."

Gain of Past Experience

"India should not transport the shortcomings of other nations. India must gain from its [own] experiences of the past."

Thinking for Progress

"What India needs to progress that it already has. But, its own internal situations have choked the way of its progress; and each and every Indian should think over it seriously."

Need of Difference

"If we want to understand a subject clearly then it is essential for us that we know the difference between the Past and Present."

Analysis of Principle

"All the theories or practices, general or natural, are the subject of analysis. It is the demand of good sense that the principle should be brought to the acid test and the process of analysis."

Sense of Naturalness

"There is no sense of accepting a thing to be natural without proper analysis."

Opened Mind Discussion

"As remedies we can expect good and fruitful consequences only if our thoughts are open minded. Being stubborn and orthodox is not a good sign of intelligence. Nobody can find out a remedy in doing so. This is rather more important in the social sphere."

Complain

"A person if complains usually experiences woes and difficulties."

Blessing of Gandhi

"The abolition of Salt Tax was done in memory of Mr. Gandhi. I respect him. After all, Untouchables, according to all of us, were nearest and dearest to him. [So] there is no reason why Mr. Gandhi may not bless this project of [Scheduled Caste] from heaven."

Value of Property

"We can say that it is not a fault of the property rather it is of subject-distribution. For example those who do not possess the property they try to step forward on the path of destruction to obtain it as compared to those who already possess that."

Secret of Development

"Those who strive always progress. Some keeping a wrong impression that they cannot progress. But remember always that the days of helplessness are fading away. The days of past have gone and now you are capable of achieving according to your potential."

Surge and Constructiveness

"Every surge if not obstructed will produce anew; it is however another thing that the use of originated thing will be feasible or not!"

Responsibility on Shoulders

"Taking the responsibility upon our own shoulders we should do whatever we can to mitigate our curses."

Well-Use of Opp`ortunity

"If you will not take proper advantage of opportunity [accorded to you], there will be no end to your difficulties. I am afraid the slavery for which we are fighting will tighten us again and [in such a situation] our awakening will not last long."

Sin and Immorality

"Immorality and sin cannot be tolerated because most [of the people] have become accustomed to it, or they like it."

Collective Use

"A thing that is achieved through collected efforts cannot not be of an individual use alone; or an individual [alone] cannot claim on it."

Illiterate People

"No illiterate, superstitious and ignorant group of the people can select the right leadership."

Regular Struggle

"At the time of struggle to establish national awareness and equal nationality [in India we] should not indulge in an act that weakens this struggle or makes it lifeless."

Gift of Englishmen

"The one of the two things of Englishmen, which I am generous enough to admit, is that they have done for us a common code of law. You can travel from Kashmir down to South India and know that murder is the same thing whether you commit it in Kashmir, in Punjab or in Madras... The other thing that the British have done is that they have given us a common Central Government. Such a thing we did not have before. The importance of this fact of having a common Central Government was not probably realized by us."

Personal Gain

"I have not taken the course to individual gain. If I would have done so then I would have been at some other place."

Loyalty of Untouchables

"I will not keep the countrymen in any doubt about another loyalty...I am bound to this loyalty and cannot give it up. This loyalty remains towards the Community of Untouchables where I were born; I live there and I hope that I will never leave it."

Secularism

"In the secular, as distinguished from the religious field, every matter is a matter of general concern to all."

Mao Tse-Tung

"We should not depend upon the ***Panchasheela*** accepted by Mao [Tse-Tung]. If Mao would have any faith in the ***Panchasheela***, which is the essential part of Buddhism, he certainly would treat the Buddhists of his own country in a different way."

Way to Understanding

"The best way to understand a thing is its comparison [with the other] and reversal."

End of Impurity

"Impurity with the passage of time does not end itself; to finish impurity we must devise a scheme at certain time."

Conclusion of Alliance

"The conclusion of an alliance remains in the fact that a unit by protecting its right to withdraw [from the alliance] can return to its original state."

Public Responsibility

"It is the duty of the people to change a Government that has not been able to perform its responsibility and has not passed its acid test in prescribed time.

Swarajya to be Welcomed

"I will welcome that ***Swarajya*** which along with working on the principle of majority ascertains co-operation and consent of the minorities. Without the co-operation and consent of minorities no rule can become the self-rule [***Swarajya***], no matter if some sound arguments are given in this regard."

Collective Activities

"As much as the opportunities for collective activities are created it will be good [in the public interest], because in such a situation at the large scale anew socialization will be there and resultantly groups and Castes will abolish sharply."

Outcome of Act

"The man who comes to kill you, or to outrage the modesty of a woman, or set fire to another's house, or commits theft and is killed while struggling to escape, dies by his own sins as all aggressors and wicked men do."

Depressed Women

"If the women belonging to Depressed Communities after discharging their duties at home could spare some time for the work to be done for the welfare of their own people, they too can contribute to service of the Community."

Dignity of Community

"People belonging to Scheduled Castes should not side with the Nizam of Hyderabad, who is the enemy of country, and bring disgrace upon their community."

Quality and Level

"As per the common feeling it cannot be accepted that those who are in the existence through the ages, they are improving and progressing. [In fact] importance does not remain in the existence; it remains in the quality of existence and status."

Source of Power

"*Dharma*, social status and wealth- all these are the source of power and authority."

Public Monument

"No individual can establish his control over a public monument."

Secret of Influence

"If you want to be effective then it is not possible only on the strength of polite viewpoint. For, you should be ready...and should have enough strength to fight according to situation."

Expenditure Accomplishment

"If during the course of war you [the rich] have no objection to pay extra [taxes] then why you should object to the fund to be collected with the purpose of welfare of labourer or to improve their standard of living."

Progress and Efforts

"Activity is the condition of growth; for, work is necessary if there is a desire to progress."

Noble Literature

"For the noble literature in no condition the honour and [self] respect of man can be allowed to lose. The causes of such a situation are those social grounds that make it peculiar on the one hand, and they [also] make it unnatural on the other."

Use of Power

"At the time of using the force with the purpose of obtaining a thing we should see that the use of it be constructive and not as the misuse to provocation the violence."

Creation of History

"They cannot make histories who forget history."

Liberation of Self

"Devotion can be a way to liberation of self; but in politics the devotion or worship of leader is certainly a way to falling down and also to despotism."

East and West

"The East is ever eager to give prominence to terms of self-globalization to one-that of its being free from the extreme materialism of the West leading to war and devastation."

Value of Progress

"The good things of this earth do not fall from heaven. Every progress has its bill of its costs and only those who pay for it will have that progress."

Taxation

"The first and most essential requirement of a good revenue system is that it should be reliable. It does not matter whether that revenue system brings in large revenue or small revenue."

Devotion and Goal

"The things that cause to shake our determination and belief and put us at a distance to our goal should be considered as the curse; and they of course cannot be the boon."

Honour of Self-Respect

"To agree to a price for a few pieces of bread or to surrender rights, or to lose self-respect for some temporary gain in no way is graceful."

Constructive Nature

"Both-the constructive tendency and the taking tendency- possess different levels. Certainly, the methods of development of the constructive tendency and of decline of the other are different. Nothing is such thing that the development of the one is the decline of the other."

Selected System

"We want such a system in which not only our [human] rights are with us, but we also have the right to bring the people of our Community in the [Legislative] House to take part in the discussion that takes place there and they also become the part of every decision."

****

"It is the duty of the Legislature to provide for your food, clothes, shelter, education, medicine and all the means of earning a livelihood. The work of law-making and of its execution is to be performed with your consent, help and will. In short, law is the abode of all worldly happiness."

-Bhimrao Ambedkar

CHRONOLOGY OF EVENTS

Year Month Date		Event
1891 April 14	:	Birth at Mhow Cantonment [of Madhya Pradesh of the day]; Father: Ramji Sakpal, who originally was a resident of Ambavade village in Ratnagiri District of the Konkan Region, and at the time of Bhimrao's birth was posted at Mhow as a ***Subedar*** in the Army; Maloji Sakpal, the father of Ramji Sakpal, belonged to a well-known Mahar family, dedicated to ***Karuna***-the compassion, ***Maitri***-the friendliness and other human values, and had faith in the teachings and preaching of Saint Kabir; Mother: Bhimabai belonged to a family of Murbad village in the Thane District [***Navi Mumbai***] and her father and six uncles were ***Subedar***-Majors in the Indian Army; Bhimabai's family too had faith in the teachings and preaching of Saint Kabir; Bhimrao was the 14th child of the parents and that is why he was affectionately called the 14th ***Ratna***.

1896 : After retirement, father Ramji Sakpal came down to Dapoli in the Central India where Bhimrao was put to school for his primary education, but due to some inconveniences, Ramji Ambedkar could not stay at Dapoli and moved to Mumbai and from there to Satara.

1897 : Mother Bhimabai passed away in Satara; paternal aunt Mirabai took special care of Bhimrao after his mother's death; father Ramji Sakpal too started paying more attention towards Bhim and other children, he used to read and recite to the children the epics, and introduced to them the spiritual Marathi songs of saints like Moropant, Mukteshwar and Tukaram; as Ramji Sakpal himself had a long teaching experience while serving in the Army and had been a head-master for 14 years, he himself became the first teacher of his children; Bhim and other children attended primary school at Satara also.

1907	:	Passed the Matriculation Examination from Elphinstone High School of Mumbai; in a public function organized under the Chairmanship of S. K. Bole, Bhimrao was publicly honoured for his good performance in the Matriculation Examination; wedded to Rami, who after her marriage with Bhimrao, as per the tradition, was renamed Ramabai; honouring the desire of his father, Ramji, Bhimrao again joined Elphinstone College in Mumbai for higher studies.
1909	:	Commented on the Morley-Minto Reforms [Scheme].
1912	:	Passed his B. A. Examination securing the first class; he also topped the list of successful candidates; joined the State Service of Baroda.
1913 February 2	:	Father Ramji Sakpal died in Mumbai; with financial support of the Maharaja of Baroda, Bhimrao decided to go to the Columbia University, U.S.A. for higher studies.
1915	:	Earned Master Degree for his research work entitled, "Ancient Indian Commerce."

1916 June	:	Obtained the Degree of Doctor of Philosophy from the University of Columbia for his thesis entitled, "***National Dividend of India: A Historic and Analytic Study***"; entered to the Grays Inn for the study of law and the London School of Economic and Politics for the study of economics.
1917 August 21	:	Reached Mumbai; was accorded a grand public welcome on his great academic achievements; decided to go to Baroda to join the service of Maharaja; became victim of ill-treatment in the State of Baroda; November: resigned from the Baroda State Service and reached Mumbai; started work of private-teaching and advising merchants about shares.
1918	:	Wrote two articles of highest standard under the titles, "***Castes in India***" and "***Small Holdings in India and Their Remedies***", and became successful in attracting attention of intelligentsia of the country; was appointed a professor of political economy at the Sydenham College

		of Commerce and Economics in Mumbai.
1919	:	Came in close contact of Shahuji Maharaj, the illustrious prince of Kolhapur.
1920 January 31	:	Started a fortnightly under the title, "***Mook- Nayak***"; March 21: presided over a conference of the Untouchables in Kolhapur; May: spoke in the first All-India Conference of Untouchables held at Nagpur under the Presidentship of Shahuji Maharaj of Kolhapur; October: resumed studies in economics after his arrival in London.
1921	:	Met Montagu, then Secretary of State for India and Vithalbhai Patel and discussed about difficulties and grievances of the Indian Untouchables with them.
1922 April-May	:	Visited Germany and tried to enter the University of Bonn.
1923 April	:	Returned to Mumbai and from there re-submitted his thesis entitled, "***The Problem of the Rupee***" to the London School of Economics and Politics; was awarded the Degree of

		Doctor of Science by the L. S. E. P.
1924 July 20	:	With the efforts of Bhimrao Ambedkar the "***Bahishkrit Hitakarini Sabha***" was founded under the Chairmanship of Chimanlal Hiralal Setalvad; Bhimrao Ambedkar himself became the Chairman of the Managing Committee of the ***Sabha***.
1925 January 4	:	The ***Bahishkrit Hitakarini Sabha*** started a hostel at Sholapur for students belonging to Depressed Classes.
1927 May	:	Was nominated to the Bombay Legislative Council; July: addressing a huge gathering in Pune, Ambedkar made demand of equal rights for Depressed and Untouchables; August-December: led a struggle for use of ***Mahad Tank*** for the Untouchables.
1929 April-May	:	Opposed the call to Strike given by the Communists in the textile-mills because the Communist leaders had never raised their voice in favour of the ***Dalits***.

1930 March	:	Started ***Satyagraha*** for the restoration of right of ***Dalits*** to enter in the [Hindu] temples; became a representative of Depressed Classes to participate in the "***First Round Table Conference***" convened in London.
1931 August 14	:	Had meeting with Mahatma Gandhi in the Manibhavan, Mumbai; proceeded to London to attend the "***Second Round Table Conference***".
1932 February 28	:	Was accorded a grand welcome in the City of Madras; traveled to England, met Ministers and British Premier in London; September 24: signed the "Poona Pact".
1936 January	:	Wrote his famous article on Caste System [in India]; visited England.
1937 February	:	Elected to the Bombay Legislative Assembly; August: became the President and Treasurer of [newly founded] Independent Labour Party; September: presented a Bill in the Bombay Legislative Assembly to abolish the "***Khoti System***."

1939	:	Opposed the British proposal of a Federal System for India; October: had talks with Nehru in Mumbai.
1941 July	:	was appointed a Member to the Defence Advisory Council of the Viceroy.
1942	:	Rejected the Cripps Proposals; March: organized the ***Dalit Conference***; July: became a Member of the Viceroy's Council.
1943 May 7	:	Presided over the Labour Conference in Mumbai.
1945 November 27	:	Presided over the 7th Labour Conference held in Delhi; visited Southern parts of India.
1946 April 5	:	Met the Members of the Cabinet Mission Plan; June 20: founded the ***Jana-Shiksha Samiti*** [Public Education Society]; elected to the [Indian] Constituent Assembly from Bengal.
1947 July	:	Re-elected to the Constituent Assembly by the Bombay Legislative Assembly; became the Chairman of the Drafting Committee of the

		Constituent Assembly; August 3: Ambedkar's name appeared in the list of Members of the First Cabinet for the free India to be lead by Pt. Nehru; 15: became the Union Law Minister.
1949 November 25	:	Replied all questions, raised by the Members, during the course of an open debate in the Constituent Assembly as the Chief Architect of the Constitution.
1950 January 26	:	Was included in the First Cabinet of the Republic of India.
1952 March	:	Elected to the Rajya Sabha.
1953 January 12	:	The Honourary Degree of the D. Litt. was conferred on Babasaheb Dr. Bhimrao Ambedkar by the Osmania University of Hyderabad; dedicated his life for the propagation of the Buddhism.
1954	:	Criticized the working method and policy of Mao Tse-Tung while speaking in the Rajya Sabha on Indo-China relations and the foreign policy; demanded immediate action in Goa and its merger with the Union of India;

October 3: speaking on the All-India Radio Babasaheb Ambedkar emphasized upon equality and equality-based society.

1956 October 14 : Converted to Buddhism; 15: was accorded civil welcome by the Municipal Corporation of Nagpur; December 2: participated in the function organized in Delhi to accord welcome to the Dalai Lama; 6: passed away in Delhi in the early hours [around 6 a.m.]; was cremated in Mumbai.

****